To Althea
Peace

Bernadette Moss

From the Heart

A POETIC AUTOBIOGRAPHY

Bernadette Moss

From the Heart
Copyright © 2022 Bernadette Moss

ISBN: 978-1-954517-25-7

All rights reserved. No part of this book may be reproduced in any form or by any electronic or mechanical means, including information storage and retrieval systems, without permission in writing from the author, except by a reviewer, who may quote brief passages in review.

Designed and produced by:
Indie Author Books
12 High Street, Thomaston, Maine
www.indieauthorbooks.com

Printed in the United States of America

To my family and the communities that nurtured me

The Ways of the Child

She just won't take a nap,
    won't settle down,
        might miss some talk or a laugh.

She's precocious as the day is new.
    Solves one problem
while creating two.

Never misses a trick,
    always alert,
    on guard,
    watching with her heart.

Always a challenge,
    stubborn,
    but somehow right,
    stays with a thought long into the night.

The world is hers.
    Confident,
    strong,
    she steps up to claim it.
    Turns around,
    seeks to share it.

Will you welcome the child?
    or turn her away?
    One fair warning.
    Rejected yesterday, she'll be here today.

Homeless Shelter

I wouldn't want to have to live here.
    But she does have
        to live here, alone,
        perhaps with a child.

Maybe her husband beat her, or just left...
        she's just like the other homeless,
        alone. Borrowed bed, plastic forks,
        spam three times a week. Somehow
        it beats the street; especially with
        the child.

I wouldn't want these dingy walls, torn and mended upholstery,
        cracked plastic couches. Oh but yes, notice swept floors,
        straightened cubicles, laughing children sharing toys.

How comforting as I leave her home to go back to mine. I've done my part,
        promised ten percent of what I earn and pieces of my heart.
        It hurts. It's what I learned.

Healing

Nothing's wrong, some things 're right.
can't say life's been always so kind, or if I like it without the fight.
    From early on I met with success,
    resolving conflicts, managing stress.
    It came to be what I did best.
Out from the alcoholic home
    I took my skills so finely honed.
And in the world I was blest
    with opportunity to resolve conflict and manage stress.
Crisis to crisis I was swept along,
    always scared but forever strong.
'Til one, piled on the heap too high,
    led to my rather tragic demise.
It took ten years but now I see,
    I always have options open to me.
Some days I choose a path that's right,
    filled with peace, joy, and light.
Other days I choose to reminisce
    the times of conflict and managing stress.

Doing Life

Sunlight signals yet another day.
    Warily I check the chains that bid me stay.

Probing gently, I slowly go
        through my mind
                from head to toe.

The verdict in, I draw a breath.
    Today I'll give my pillow a rest.

I'll choose to experience what lies ahead,
        while honoring my fear;
                stopping short of dread

Stepping out in faith,
        I meet with peace,
                a little anger,
                      then some joy.

And through it all, I am safe.

Doug

"He loves me, he loves me not."
    Since we've met, I've put aside such silly games,
to focus on what I've got.

Tall of stature, your shoulders broad;
    Not seeking, but willing to accept, the heavy load.
Your gentle eyes a vision see;
    same steady eyes that see through me.

Laughter from your lips peals heartily
    echoes off my heart, causing me to be still.
Oh God! How I love your laugh. How I love you.
    Know that I always will.

An Untitled Thank you

Someone saw beyond or perhaps
didn't choose to see,
physical limitations that kept me 20 years
staring at, but not on, the sea.

Come, she invites.
High tide, my boat is ready.
Want to try?

Make your mark, manage the waves;
they're indiscriminate, not caring about failing body parts:
off balance, bone scraping bone—the neck, the knee,
heart congested, beats steady,
Leave the shore behind?

I pause;
pain be damned! toss my cane to the dock
I breathe, then drop.
Her hard wood welcoming my damaged goods.

Gwen takes the tiller. Paul pulls up the sail. I take it in. It comes back,
we speak the
language I remember.

Here.
The tiller finds my hand. Want to steer?
My chance.
A stab at life not too kind.
Torn up body, fighting hell to salvage mind.

I never guessed; always knew I'd find myself, not lost, again at sea.
A dream being made to happen.
I inhale.
I breathe.

Communication

"Say something," he demanded. "What's on your mind?"

Opportunity unleashed an outburst. Words hammered hard,
                                                  hitting at
                                                                    hurts inflicted

Casually, and expected to be forgotten
                                    before they were felt.

"My God," he reflected silently,
                        "is that all she cares about?"

Forget your damn delicate feelings for once,
                                    he longed to scream.

Trapped by the torrent he had triggered,
          he retreated
                      inward
                              unaware of a sudden silence.

"Say something," she demanded. "What's on your mind?"

Unborn Child

No my child you can not come.
    You would not be safe.
    You would come to harm.
I have a sickness I did not choose.
    It is my choice however,
        to protect you.
Love transcends the loss I bear;
    not to hear you laugh,
        our love to share.
I know you want to see this
    world,
        and I,
            you.
But it would not be the way you trust.
    I couldn't promise that love
        would be enough.
I'd like to tell you wait awhile,
    but I won't deceive you.
Forgive me my child.
No my child you can not come.
    You would not be safe.
    You would come to harm.

Bi-Polar

I'm back. You ask, from where?
Another planet, another world.
Don't know how I got here, don't remember packing for the trip.
I remember feet planted on the ground, legs, arms, head.
    They stayed there too.
My mind? Ah! That's different.
Some trips are by invitation, others just happen. This was one of those.
I didn't go very far. Oh? But did I tell you it was good? Would you agree.
It was good to leave behind the mundane, to become unfettered,
    to burst through smothered
potential. Greater, to annihilate averageness.
The trip. The excursion away from ordinary, was beyond good.
    To write it down would
make it ordinary.
It doesn't matter. I'm back.
My feet, still planted on the ground. Legs, arms, head, now mind,
    connected like the dots.
I wasn't temped to stay in that place too long. First the illusion it's free.
    Later the ticket
collector reaching out.
No thank you.
So I'm back. To life familiar, to the despised averageness, to the mundane,
to the ordinary, to the steady, the best part, to you.

Gratitude

It's scary Lord to praise your name,
    I owe You so much I'll do it just the same.

You knew at my birth much pain was in store,
    that over my wounds Your love You would pour.

You gave me a mother named for your own,
    who like Your's stood in my times alone.

Others You sent my way as well,
    saving me Lord from a life turned hell.
    Manic depression is my cross to bear, like Calvary
    repeated I know You've been there.

While You rose to heaven, my time hasn't come.
    I believe then there's still work to be done.
Laughter, peace, joy and song:
    these are Your gifts Lord that will bring me home...

But while in this world, let me never forget;
    that in friend, as in stranger, You and I have met.

The Thief

Why Can't I go home?

What's wrong Mama? Don't you like it here?
        Thoughtfully,
It's not about liking. It's longing. To be where I was, how I was.
Bernadette. Tell me why I can't go home.

Well, you've gained a lot of weight. It's the medicine to help your lungs.
It's not your fault. You need help to get up. Walking is hard.
You don't want to break a hip?

Can't somebody go with me? All the time?
    To walk with me, where I need to go?

No Mama, that can't happen. The aides come for a short time, mostly for showers. Some you won't like. You'll refuse.

Oh! I wouldn't complain. It's their job. I'm a nurse. I know.

Of course you know: as long as you're saying the words. You'll forget. Dementia does that. It's not your fault. We'd love to have you home, for sure. With you downstairs I'd see you every day—between my job and cooking, cleaning upstairs with Doug. As for Bob, no more winding night trips home. He'd be living there, with you—most of the time—but there'd be banking, picking up pills, grocery shopping, other errands. You'd think sometimes he wasn't coming back. Honest, you would. But it's not your fault
        Mom, firmly,

Well. It is what it is.

I wish you could come home Mama. I don't like that you're living here, even if nothing is wrong. Then it's not about liking. It's longing for you to be where you were, how you were.

Thank You Lord for Loving Me

I know others put it differently Lord,
    but this song comes from my heart.
It skips a beat. It almost stops
    from time to time but starts,
    with gratitude and love for You
    to praise and thank you
            for all of me.

This prayer, these words, come Lord,
    straight from You.
My part I discern,
    is to listen to the
Spirit who is sent
    by You.

So Lord I ask,
    and know that I'll receive,
an ear fine tuned
    to the music You play.
A heart of love, a soul of peace.
Joy at knowing
        that
            You'll never leave.

A Prayer

I feel Your voice deep in my soul.

What is your plan?
    How will I know?
        Should I wait, the answer to unfold?

Could it be through poems, words yet untold?

Call to my heart,
    I'll choose to obey.

When I listen,
    I'll know how to share
        the love you give, Lord,
            how much you care.

Ask Me

Lord I love You there is no doubt
what you want.
Sometimes I'll say yes.
    If we argue You'll always win out.
Arguing is foolish, You know what is best.
What stands in the way?
    My humanness.

Abundance

A poem is a gift from above,
    Given to share your heartfelt love.

Nature beckons it's wonders exceed
    bugs, bees, butterflies
beneath a breathless, treeless sky—blue.

Clouds linger lightly
    sun dancing through.

Blossoming flowers grace the land,
    singing to the keeper of nature.

All is safe in His hands.

Hospice

Life is a journey, love leads the
way. You to eternity, me to stay.

Tears trickle down my face;
his hand brushes them away.
A smile in his eyes, sadness
in his face.

Come now, the ocean waits.
Your place is home, I'll
be there. You are not alone.

God's Umbrella

Shelter me Lord from any
storm.
From days turned down, then
up—to be found in your arms
Love lights my path, tears
the shade.
I grieve; the gift you gave
no longer alive.
Yours to give, Yours to take.
My life goes on. Alone.
Shelter me Lord from this
storm.

Waiting

Grief knows no time or place.

In love. Missing him. Being alone.

One journey, my journey, finds me
by the sea

Mirror-like ocean calms, sun warms.

Near-by, red maple's gentle breeze
inspires a song

Softly, memories filter thru life's mystery

One called. I wait—on my own.

A stranger's smile, a wave. I'm not alone.

A Glimpse of Heaven

On the porch waiting.
Sunset. A splash of red, yellow, green
above the sea.
        Watching
Boats easy rocking, ocean gently pushing
            waves
                  slapping ships minus sails on
a forgiving sea.
Something more?
No speaks the ocean breeze...
        Heaven meets earth.
        Paradise in between.

Letting Go

There's never a "good" time to pass,
    leaving loved ones in tears,
        still able to laugh.

It's time to leave, to say goodbye,
    my body's wasted, but not my mind.

Take my hand,
    hold me close.

You'll join me when it's your time.

Courage

Grief lingers, two years he's gone.

My heart speaks: don't cry

Love keeps him alive,
    yet now a spirit,
        not one I can hold.

Courage signals,
    be in it for the long, difficult haul.

This thought was new, though I'd been forewarned.

His body weakened,
    life leaving,
        I'd be on my own.

While his body sleeps, his spirit soars.

I find him opening not one but many doors.

Expecting change, life comes to me slowly, but comes along,
    easing a fear I won't name.

Who knows—is it being alone?

Calling on a need to be strong—I claim his spirit.

    Love lives on.